A Curriculum Guide for

Axle Galench and

The Gate of No Return

By Rooster Morris

Curriculum written by
Cyndy Unwin, Ph.D.

ISBN 0-9755895-0-4

Table of Contents

Learning Objectives

❖ Students apply a wide range of strategies to comprehend, interpret, evaluate, and appreciate texts.

❖ Students employ a wide range of strategies as they write and use different writing process elements appropriately to communicate with different audiences for a variety of purposes.

❖ Students apply knowledge of language structure, language conventions, media techniques, figurative language, and genre to create, critique, and discuss print and nonprint texts.

❖ Students participate as knowledgeable, reflective, creative, and critical members of a variety of literacy communities.

Taken from the National Standards for the English Language Arts

About the Author

Rooster Morris
Author, Entertainer, Musician & Composer

Rooster Morris grew up living the cowboy life. At the age of five, Rooster began riding horses and working cattle with his father on ranches in the tri-state area of Texas, New Mexico and Oklahoma. Living in remote places, Rooster developed a unique way of entertaining himself. He started imitating bird calls and coyotes howling, then began working on voices. Little did he know that many years later, the skills he taught himself would result in recording audio books with different voice characterizations.

Rooster's musical skills are self-taught as well. He began learning to play the fiddle when he was a teenager. By the time he graduated from high school, he was playing for the historic Western Cowpunchers Association that was established in the 1880's in Amarillo, Texas. He has since been recorded by the Smithsonian Institute playing old-time fiddle music, recorded a CD of his original compositions, and taught himself how to play guitar, mandolin, and bass.

While opening for a children's author at an event in Lubbock, Texas, Rooster was deeply moved by the response of the children to the readings and songs and to the enthusiasm displayed after the show. Rooster decided to spend the next few weeks reading children's books and writing songs that he could perform for students. He spent the next five years touring the United States performing for students, teachers, librarians, and civic organizations, bringing the joy of reading and performing to over two million people. His talent, combined with a passion for performing, has inspired and encouraged children to read. This experience is what led Rooster to begin writing his own book. His desire is for kids of all ages to enjoy reading.

So, Rooster went to work writing and spent two years on his first book, *Axle Galench and the Gate of No Return*, which was released in both book and audio form in the fall of 2004. This is the first book in a series for readers in third grade and up. Reviewers are calling *Gate of No Return* "riveting, compelling, playful, and absolutely hilarious."

Rooster Morris was born in Ridgecrest, California, on September 16, 1955. He currently resides in Perryton, Texas, where he is working on the third Axle Galench book, *Axle Galench and the Spin Lizard Rescue*.

Axle Galench and the Gate of No Return
Curriculum Alignment
Texas Essential Knowledge and Skills (TEKS)

110.6. English Language Arts and Reading, Grade 4
110.7. English Language Arts and Reading, Grade 5

Note: Objectives are identical for each grade with the exception of 7B (fifth graders are expected to read 100 wpm as opposed to 90 wpm) and 15G (fifth graders are expected to begin using literary devices correctly in their writing)

Pre-reading activities:

1A, 4A, 5A, 5F, 6C, 9C, 9D, 11A, 11D, 13B, 14A, 15A, 21B

Chapter 1:

1A, 1B, 4A, 5A, 6A, 7B, 7C, 7D, 8A, 8B, 8C, 9B, 10A, 10B, 10C, 10D, 10K, 10L, 11A, 11B, 11C, 11D, 12H, 12I, 14A, 15A, 15C, 21B

Chapter 2:

1A, 1B, 4A, 5A, 6A, 7B, 7C, 7D, 8A, 8B, 8C, 9B, 10A, 10B, 10C, 10D, 10H, 10K, 11A, 11B, 11C, 11D, 12A, 12H, 12I, 14A, 15A, 15C

Chapter 3:

1A, 1B, 4A, 5A, 6A, 7B, 7C, 7D, 8A, 8B, 8C, 9B, 10A, 10B, 10C, 10E, 10H, 10K, 11A, 11B, 11C, 11D, 12A, 12C, 12D, 12H, 12I, 14A, 15A, 15C, 15F, 16A, 16B, 17C, 17D, 18B, 18C, 19A, 19B, 19C, 19D, 19E, 19F, 19H, 19I, 20D, 25B

Chapter 4:

1A, 1B, 4A, 5A, 6A, 7B, 7C, 7D, 8A, 8B, 8C, 9B, 10A, 10B, 10C, 10D, 10H, 10K, 11A, 11B, 11C, 11D, 12A, 12H, 12I, 14A, 15A, 15C

Chapter 5:

1A, 1B, 4A, 5A, 5B, 5D, 5E, 6A, 7B, 7C, 7D, 8A, 8B, 8C, 9B, 10A, 10B, 10C, 10D, 10E, 10F, 10K, 10L, 11A, 11B, 11C, 11D, 12H, 12I, 14A, 15A, 15C, 15F

Chapter 6:

1A, 1B, 4A, 5A, 6A, 7B, 7C, 7D, 8A, 8B, 8C, 9B, 10A, 10B, 10C, 10D, 10H, 10K, 11A, 11B, 11C, 11D, 12A, 12H, 12I, 14A, 15A, 15C

Chapter 7:

1A, 1B, 3B, 3C, 4A, 5A, 6A, 7B, 7C, 7D, 8A, 8B, 8C, 9B, 10A, 10B, 10C, 10H, 10K, 11A, 11B, 11C, 11D, 12A, 12H, 12I, 12J, 14A, 15A, 15C, 15D, 15F

15G (grade 5 only)

Chapter 8:

1A, 1B, 4A, 5A, 6A, 7B, 7C, 7D, 8A, 8B, 8C, 9B, 10A, 10B, 10C, 10H, 10K, 11A, 11B, 11C, 11D, 12A, 12H, 12I, 14A, 15A, 15C, 15D, 15E, 15F, 16A, 16B, 17C, 17D, 18B, 18C, 18D, 20B

Chapter 9:

1A, 1B, 4A, 5A, 6A, 7B, 7C, 7D, 8A, 8B, 8C, 9B, 10A, 10B, 10C, 10D, 10K, 10L, 11A, 11B, 11C, 11D, 12H, 12I, 14A, 15A, 15C, 21B

Chapter 10:

1A, 1B, 3A, 3C, 4A, 5A, 5C, 5D, 6A, 7B, 7C, 7D, 8A, 8B, 8C, 9B, 10A, 10B, 10C, 10D, 10F, 10H, 10K, 11A, 11B, 11C, 11D, 12A, 12B, 12H, 12I, 12J, 14A, 15A, 15C, 15D, 15F

15G (grade 5 only)

Chapter 11:

1A, 1B, 4A, 5A, 6A, 6B, 7B, 7C, 7D, 8A, 8B, 8C, 9B, 9C, 10A, 10B, 10C, 10K, 10L, 11A, 11B, 11C, 11D, 12H, 12I, 14A, 15A, 15C, 21B

Chapter 12:

1A, 1B, 4A, 5A, 6A, 7B, 7C, 7D, 8A, 8B, 8C, 9B, 10A, 10B, 10C, 10E, 10F, 10G, 10K, 10L, 11A, 11B, 11C, 11D, 12B, 12H, 12I, 12J, 14A, 15A, 15C, 21B

Post-Reading Enrichment:

9B, 10E, 10G, 10H, 10K, 11A, 11B, 11D, 12H, 12I, 15A, 15C, 15D, 15F, 16A, 16B, 17C, 17D, 18B, 18C, 19A, 19B, 19C, 19D, 19E, 19F, 19H, 19I, 20C

Pre-Reading Activities

Discussion Starters:

- ❖ Describe a time when you've felt different from everyone else. How did you feel inside?
- ❖ Is there anything about your parents that you think sets them apart from other parents? If so, what?
- ❖ Describe a world in which everything is orderly. What would it be like to live in that world? What would school be like?

Group Activity:

In groups of three or four, draw sketches and write simple descriptions of an imaginary world in which everything was orderly. Share these ideas with your classmates. Save your work on this project for later!

Vocabulary Development:

- ❖ Fold 7 sheets of blank white paper in half, hamburger-style, and cover with a folded sheet of construction paper. Staple or tie all the pages together along the edge. Write the following title on the cover: *The Language of Kamoo and Other New and Interesting Words.* Beginning with "A," write one letter of the alphabet at the top of each page. As the story progresses, write each word unique to Kamoo or new to you on the page that corresponds with its first letter. Illustrate the cover and pages of the dictionary with pictures from the events in the story.

- ❖ <u>Order</u> and <u>disorder</u> are opposites. Look these words up in the dictionary and write their definitions. Then, fill in the T-Chart on the next page with five examples each of orderly and disorderly things. An example has been provided for you.

Pre-Reading Vocabulary **Name:**________________

Directions: Write 5 examples each of orderly and disorderly things on the T-Chart below.

Order	Disorder
My teenage sister's perfectly straight hair	My bedhead in the morning

Chapter 1

Questions for Discussion

Name: _____

1. Draw a diagram or picture that shows how the following terms relate to each other: Mizmoe, Kamoo, Bedlam, and Manarkin.

2. How are Earth and Mizmoe alike and different?

3. Do you think Axle is a typical Manarkin? Why or why not? What events in the story so far lead you to feel this way?

4. What do you think happened to Axle's father?

Directions: In the middle circles, write the similarities between humans and Manarkins. In the upper and lower circles, write the differences.

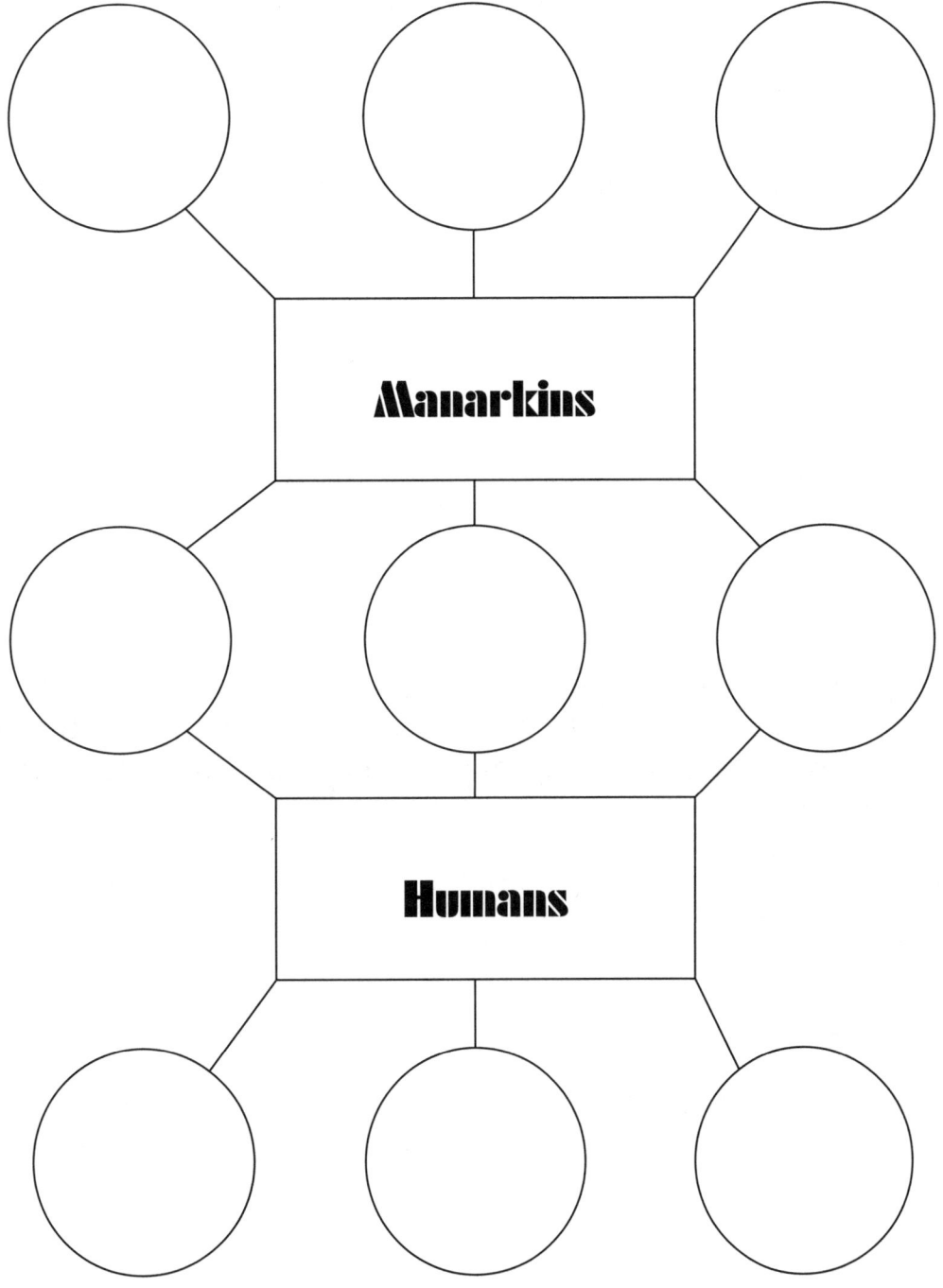

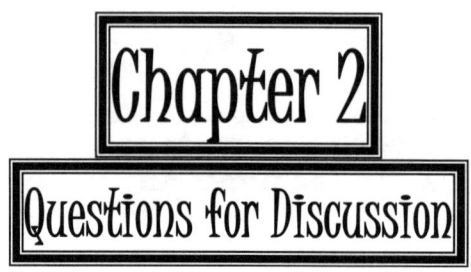

Chapter 2

Questions for Discussion

Name: _____

1. When Axle is sent to the principal's office, Mr. Moof tells him that his misbehavior in class is the "needle that broke the camel's haystack." What other things has Axle done to get himself in trouble? What two figures of speech (or *idioms*) did Mr. Moof combine to come up with the one that confused Axle so much?

2. Axle has feelings of uneasiness in this chapter. Find all the places where he mentions these feelings and write the words from the story here. What do you think they mean?

3. What are your predictions about what Clea was going to tell Axle about the ring on her finger?

Mental Image Drawing

Directions: One of the best ways to comprehend what we read is make mental pictures of the scenes and events in our mind. Re-read the section of Chapter 2 that describes what Kamoo looks like as Axle walks to the council building to speak to the judge. In the space below, draw the image or picture you had in your mind as you read. After you're finished, compare your drawing to a classmate's.

Chapter 3
Questions for Discussion

Name: _____

1. Describe what happened to Axle after he dropped the ring.
    Why did the crowd react as it did?

2. How would you respond if you suddenly changed form and
    became some other type of creature? If you could be anything
    but human, what real or imaginary creature would you choose
    to be?

3. Would you like to live in Kamoo? Why or why not?

Directions: Pretend you are a newspaper reporter who was in the courtroom listening to the judge talk to Axle. You witnessed Axle's transformation, and it is your task to write the front page story that will be published in the Kamoo newspaper the next day. Use a real newspaper as an example to help you format the article correctly, and be sure to include the 5 W's at the beginning of your news article--who, what, when, where, and why.

_____

_____

_____

_____

_____

_____

_____

_____

_____

_____

_____

_____

_____

_____

_____

_____

_____

_____

_____

_____

_____

_____

_____

_____

_____

_____

Chapter 4

Questions for Discussion

Name: _____

1. Who are the Droolsops? Why would they want the Manarkins to believe humans are poisonous?

2. What are Stewards of Balance? Why is Axle a steward? What does being a steward enable him to do?

3. Who is Nacklenod? Why is it so important that Axle find him?

4. Draw a picture of what you think the Gate of No Return (the gate in between Kamoo and Bedlam) looks like. Be sure to include the surrounding areas, too.

Chapter 4 Activity
Wanted Poster

Name: _____

Directions: In the space below, create a "Wanted" poster for Axle and Clea, to be displayed throughout Kamoo after their disappearance.

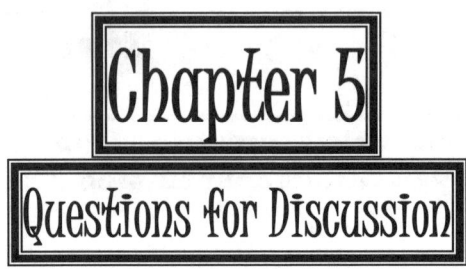

Chapter 5

Questions for Discussion

Name: _____

1. Who is the gatekeeper? Would you want him for a friend? Why or why not?

2. If you were Axle, would you go through the gate into Bedlam, or would you stay on Kamoo? Explain.

3. When Axle realized he was locked in Bedlam, he began yelling. Does any part of what he yelled sound familiar to you? Explain.

Reading Baseball

Directions: In the spaces provided below, write four factual questions from the first 5 chapters of *Axle Galench and the Gate of No Return*. The first question should be the easiest question and represents a single hit, the second will be a bit harder and represents a double hit, and so on. Your last question should be very challenging, because it represents a home run hit.

To play the game, draw a baseball diamond on the board and pool all students' questions together. Divide into two teams. Alternating teams, each student decides which level question he/she wants to answer. Each time the student answers a question correctly, he/she moves forward the corresponding number of spaces and his/her name is written under the base. When a student reaches home base, a point is scored for that team. There are no "outs" for this version of the game.

Variation: The game can be played in innings just like real baseball, with teams answering questions until they answer three incorrectly (three "outs"). The other team would then be "up to bat" and have their turn at answering questions.

Questions:

Single: _____

_____

_____

Double: _____

_____

_____

Triple: _____

_____

_____

Home Run: _____

_____

_____

Chapter 6

Questions for Discussion

Name: _____

1. Who is Flobberjaw?

2. In what ways is Flobberjaw unlikeable? In what ways is he likeable?

3. Given Axle's choice of handing over the key or possibly being eaten by Flobberjaw, what would your decision have been? Defend your answer.

Directions: Form groups of four or five students. Complete the following activities and be prepared to share them with the class.

On a piece of large paper, draw and color a detailed picture of Flobberjaw as your group sees him. Use every detail from the story, and add some of your own!

Create a rap song out of the tune Flobberjaw sings to Axle. Every member of your group should have a part, either in chanting or making the rhythm of the rap.

Chapter 7

Questions for Discussion

Name: _____

1. What are Irrit-ants? Do they resemble any creatures we have here on Earth? Which ones?

2. Describe what Axle needs to do in order to get the key back from Flobberjaw. What do you think will be his biggest challenge?

3. When Flobberjaw says, "Like that's some mo' ya' business. Ha Ha Ha! Sumoya Ha Ha Ha! I made a funny," he is making a play on words. This is also known as a _____. (Hint: The word starts with "p.")

    Write any Knock-Knock jokes you know that also use this humor technique.

Directions: Tom Swifties are a type of pun originally seen in a series of books written by Victor Appleton over 100 years ago. Tom Swift was the main character, and whenever he spoke, an adverb was added that linked what he said to how he said it. Here's an example: "I just lost my crutches," said Tom <u>lamely</u>.

Try out some of these Tom Swifties, using the word bank below.

1. "I think I'm getting the measles," said Tom _____.

2. "The sun is coming up," said Tom _____.

3. "Why don't you clean up the lawn?" Tom asked _____.

4. "I don't give a hoot," Tom said _____.

5. "I'm the new custodian," Tom said _____.

Word Bank: brightly   rakishly   sweepingly   rashly   owlishly

Use the following words to make Tom Swifties of your own:

doggedly   blindly   sourly   halfheartedly   gamely

1. _____

2. _____

3. _____

4. _____

5. _____

(Activity adapted from <u>Ideas for Teaching English in the Junior High and Middle School</u>, edited by Candy Carter and Zora Rashkis)

Chapter 8

Questions for Discussion

Name: _____

1. Who are the Splinkerjets? What are your predictions for the role (if any) they will play later in the story?

2. Write a letter from Axle to his mother. Be specific!

Directions: Sit with your group in a circle. Each person should have a copy of this handout. When your teacher says to begin, read the end of Chapter 8 (copied below) to yourself. You will then have five minutes to continue writing the story. After five minutes, your teacher will tell you to switch, and you pass your paper to the right. On the paper you receive, read what the person before you wrote, then continue his/her story for five more minutes. Continue passing every five minutes until your own original story gets back to you, then write an ending.

The dreadful sounds of heavy breathing and cumbersome footsteps were coming closer and closer....

_____

_____

_____

_____

_____

_____

_____

_____

_____

_____

_____

_____

_____

_____

_____

_____

_____

_____

_____

_____

Chapter 9

Questions for Discussion

Name: _____

1. Whose "cumbersome footsteps" were following Axle? What happened next?

2. Name all the villains we've met in the story so far. What makes a villain a villain? Why do so many stories have them?

3. Grueloc uses a sarcastic sense of humor to amuse himself and Crabster. What is sarcasm? When is it funny? When is it not so funny?

4. What do you think Axle's plan is?

Chapter 9 Activity **Name:** ____________

Creature Characteristics

Directions: Some of the creatures Axle has met so far are listed on the chart below. Down the side of the chart is a list of characteristics. For each creature, put a + in the box when the characteristics match. Add a trait of your own at the bottom!

	Flobberjaw	Splinkerjets	Crabster	Grueloc
Bad Guy				
Good Guy				
Musical				
Nasty-Tempered				
Playful				
Greedy				
Smart				
Dangerous				
Weird				

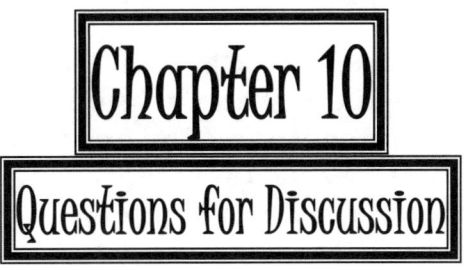

Chapter 10
Questions for Discussion

Name: _____

1. What was Axle's plan for escaping and finding the golden toadstool? How did it compare to your prediction from the end of Chapter 9?

2. Rooster Morris uses many vivid descriptions in this chapter to describe Axle and the Splinkerjets' adventures. In your opinion, what is the best description in this chapter? Why is it the best?

3. List some of the most effective descriptive words from the scene you chose in the last question OR draw the scene below.

Directions: Choose a scene from Chapter 10 you would like to act out with your group. Depending on the number of characters, two groups may need to work together. The scene should have lots of action and dialogue. Use the outline below to plan your short play. Then, practice together and perform for your class!

Page Numbers of the Scene: _____

Name of Narrator (the person who reads the words that are not spoken by the characters): _____

Character: _____ Actor: _____

Character: _____ Actor: _____

Character: _____ Actor: _____

Character: _____ Actor: _____

Character: _____ Actor: _____

Character: _____ Actor: _____

Character: _____ Actor: _____

Character: _____ Actor: _____

Props Needed: _____

Script: Rewrite the scene you chose so that it looks like a play. The narrator should introduce the scene, then each character's lines are written exactly as they are spoken in the actual story, with the "he saids" and "she saids" taken out. Put instructions for the characters in parentheses next to the character's name. The instructions are acted out, but not spoken.

Here's an example from Chapter 2:

Narrator: Axle and his mother were talking to the judge of Kamoo. The ring on Clea's finger began to burn. Axle removed the ring from his mother's finger and dropped it. The Manarkins gasped as they watched the ring roll right up to the front of the judge's desk where it stalled and began to spin in a circle. Its repetitious jingling was almost an irritation to the senses. The rotation became faster and louder. Finally and abruptly, the ringing stopped. This sudden shush left an awkward silence in the air. And in the blink of an eye, Axle felt change rushing through his body.

Axle: Mother?!

Clea: What?

Axle (quivering and shaking): I feel funny. I'm hot and cold....Something's happening!

Narrator: Suddenly Axle's body began quivering and shaking. A squealing whirlwind of brilliant-white smoke spun rapidly around his body. It gyrated faster and faster around him until it shattered with a loud BANG! Then, with a siphoned WISP!, the smoke disappeared. Wide-eyed Manarkins stood stunned. Quickly, the elderly judge came to his senses.

Judge (pointing at Axle and shouting): He's a human! Run for your lives! Don't let him touch you! Run!

Use the lines below to write a script for a play that lasts about 5 minutes.

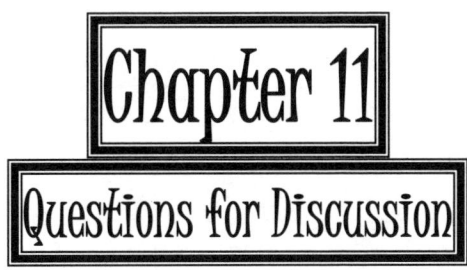

Chapter 11

Questions for Discussion

Name: _____

1. Find two examples of puns in this chapter.

2. Do you think Axle made the right decision by going back to Flobberjaw even after he lost the golden toadstool? Why or why not?

3. If you were Axle, what would you say to Flobberjaw upon meeting him? How would you convince him not to eat you once he finds out you lost the "love of his life"?

Directions: The largest five words in Chapter 11 are listed below, but they're scrambled. Without peeking back at the chapter, can you figure out what they are? Then, pick one of the words and see if you can make 50 smaller words out of it. Here's an even bigger challenge: Can you make 100 small words out of one of the big words? Good luck!

sslpniektjer

ldgaebudon

rafbolbejw

eetrdncuoen

mteciuscacrn

_____   _____   _____

_____   _____   _____

_____   _____   _____

_____   _____   _____

_____   _____   _____

_____   _____   _____

_____   _____   _____

_____   _____   _____

_____   _____   _____

_____   _____   _____

(10 words)   (10 words)   (10 words)

(20 words)

(20 words)

(20 words)

Answer Key to Word Scramble

splinkerjets
doubledang
flobberjaw
encountered
circumstance

Chapter 12

Questions for Discussion

Name: _____

1.   How do you think the golden toadstool got into the side pocket of Axle's backpack?

2.   Why did Flobberjaw refuse to give Axle the gold key? Would he have given it to him if Axle hadn't "lied"?

3.   What questions are left unanswered at the end of the story? Why do you think Rooster Morris chose to end it this way?

Directions: Divide all twelve chapters equally between groups. For each assigned chapter, groups will work together to write five answers and corresponding questions, one in each of the following Jeopardy categories: vocabulary, characters, setting (time and place), plot (story events), and Mizmoe trivia. The teacher will place the answers into Single Jeopardy and Double Jeopardy values (100 through 500 points for Single Jeopardy; 200-1000 points for Double Jeopardy). There may be a few extra answers and questions. The teacher will also decide where Daily Doubles are placed and what the Final Jeopardy question will be.

For the game, each group will play together as a team. Single Jeopardy values are written on the board under the category names. A random beginning team chooses the category and value and the answer is read (for example, "Mizmoe"). The first team to raise a hand provides the question that corresponds to the answer ("What is the planet Axle is from?"), and, if correct, wins that number of points. That team then chooses the next category and value. If a team answers incorrectly, that number of points is deducted from its total points and another team can attempt to answer. The teacher may wish to have students on the teams rotate so that only one student from each team is eligible to answer at one time. For Daily Doubles, the team choosing that answer works together to place a wager up to double the value of that answer. The team then has a set period of time to provide the question. For Final Jeopardy, the teacher names the category, then all teams place a wager up to the amount of points they have. They all then write their questions and win or lose the number of points they wagered. The team with the most points after Final Jeopardy wins.

Here is a sample Single Jeopardy playing chart:

Vocab.	Characters	Setting	Plot	Trivia
100	100	100	100	100
200	200	200	200	200
300	300	300	300	300
400	400	400	400	400
500	500	500	500	500

Post-Reading Enrichment

❖ **With your group, look at the imaginary orderly world you began to create before you read this book. Talk with each other and expand on your ideas for your world. Create a poster to share that includes descriptions of your world and illustrations to support these descriptions. Include information about the people, their customs, and the physical terrain of your world.**

❖ **Book project ideas:**

  ❖ **Design an advertising campaign to promote the reading of *Axle Galench and the Gate of No Return.***
  ❖ **Write a scene that could have happened in the book but didn't. After you have written the scene, explain how it would have changed the outcome of the book.**
  ❖ **Plan a party for the characters in the book. Design invitations, tell what food would be served, what entertainment would be provided, and how the characters would act.**
  ❖ **Using shoe boxes, make dioramas of scenes from the book, either from the land of Kamoo or from Bedlam.**

❖ **Make a Book Wheel of the events of this story. See the following handout for instructions.**

Book Wheels

Materials: Poster board, markers, brads

Directions:

1. Make two twelve-inch circles on your poster board. Both circles must be the same size. Cut out both circles.

2. Divide one circle into 8 equal wedge-shaped spaces.

3. Number each wedged space from 1-8 in a clockwise sequence. Place these numbers on the point of the wedge near the center of the circle.

4. Select 8 events from your book, evenly spaced in the beginning, middle, and end of the story.

5. Starting with wedge #1, make a colored drawing to illustrate each of the 8 events or scenes you have selected. Write a sentence on the curved edge of each wedge to explain each drawing.

6. On the other poster board circle, cut out **one** wedge the same size as the wedges on the story line circle. Do not cut the wedge all the way to the center of the circle.

7. On this wheel, write the title, author, your name, and illustrate some event or character in your book.

8. Place the cover wheel on top of the story line wheel and put the two together with a brad.

Circle 1

Circle 2

Adapted from *Effective Language Arts Techniques for Middle Grades*

by Brenda Opie and Douglas McAvinn

End-of-Novel Assessment
Axle Galench and the Gate of No Return

Name: _____

Matching: Match the word on the left with the matching phrase on the right. Write the letter of the correct answer in the space provided (2 points each).

___1.   Mizmoe   A.   The opposite of disorder

___2.   Splinkerjets   B.   The love of Flobberjaw's life

___3.   Order   C.   The planet Axle lives on

___4.   Golden toadstool   D.   The Steward of Earth

___5.   Axle Galench   E.   Has the key to the Gate of No Return

___6.   Bedlam   F.   The passageway between Kamoo and Bedlam

___7.   Flobberjaw   G.   The disorderly side of Mizmoe

___8.   Book of Equates   H.   Where Axle lived with Clea

___9.   Kamoo   I.   They love to tickle

___10. Gate of No Return   J.   Written in a secret language

Short Answer: In complete sentences, write a response to each of the following questions (15 points each).

1. Why did Axle Galench always feel uncomfortable in Kamoo?

2. What do you think Axle's greatest challenge was in this novel? Explain your reasoning.

3. Choose a character out of *Axle Galench and the Gate of No Return*. What were that character's **most** admirable qualities? What were his/her **least** admirable qualities? Would you like this character for a friend? Why or why not?

4. Write a letter to Mr. Rooster Morris, the author of this book. In the letter, tell him what you enjoyed about his book and what your suggestions would be for the rest of the books in his series.

Open Response: Complete each of these ideas with details from the book and from your own life (5 points each).

1.   This book made me wish that.....

2.   This book made me realize that.....

3.   This book made me wonder about.....

4.   This book made me hope that.....

References

Carter, C. & Rashkis, Z. (1980). *Ideas for Teaching English in the Junior High and Middle School.* Urbana, IL: National Council of Teachers of English.

Cunningham, P.M. & Hall, D.P. (1994). *Making Big Words.* Carthage, IL: Good Apple.

Fountas, I.C. & Pinnell, G.S. (2001). *Guiding Readers and Writers: Grades 3-6.* Portsmouth, NH: Heinemann.

National Council of Teachers of English and International Reading Association (1996). *Standards for the English Language Arts.* Newark, DE: IRA and NCTE.

Opie, B. & McAvinn, D. (1993). *Effective Language Arts Techniques for Middle Grades (4-8).* Marietta, GA: Masterminds Publications.

NOTES

NOTES

NOTES

NOTES